Marquis de Lafayette
and the French

Christine Dugan, M.A.Ed.

Consultant

Katie Blomquist, Ed.S.
Fairfax County Public Schools

Publishing Credits

Rachelle Cracchiolo, M.S.Ed., *Publisher*
Conni Medina, M.A.Ed., *Managing Editor*
Emily R. Smith, M.A.Ed., *Content Director*
Seth Rogers, *Editor*
Robin Erickson, *Senior Graphic Designer*

Teacher Created Materials
5301 Oceanus Drive
Huntington Beach, CA 92649-1030
http://www.tcmpub.com
ISBN 978-1-4258-6353-1
© 2017 Teacher Created Materials, Inc.

Table of Contents

An American Hero from France

In 1777, thirteen British colonies in the New World fought for their freedom. Everyone who supported the war wanted to help. Soldiers prepared to fight. Military leaders planned for battle. Others mended clothes or made weapons.

Outside the colonies, support was harder to find. People didn't know what to think about the 13 small colonies that wanted to rule themselves. Some people supported the idea but didn't believe they stood a chance against the mighty British military. Others thought the colonists were foolish to leave a country that supplied them with crucial items that they needed.

But one man knew that he needed to get involved. He was a French native and had heard about America's war with Great Britain. He volunteered to fight for a country that was not even his own.

He was the Marquis de Lafayette. A trusted friend to George Washington and Alexander Hamilton, Lafayette became a hero in America. He helped strengthen ties between France and the United States. We know his name, but who was this hero?

view of the White House from Lafayette Park

Gilbert du Motier,
Marquis de Lafayette

What's in a Name?

The Marquis de Lafayette's official birth name was Marie Joseph Paul Yves Roche Gilbert du Motier. "Marquis" is actually a title given to noblemen in some European countries.

In Honor of a Hero

Many cities, parks, and monuments around the world are named after the Marquis de Lafayette. Lafayette Park is next to the White House in Washington, D.C. The whole park is named after him!

Madame de Lafayette

Though it was an *arranged marriage*, Adrienne had a lot in common with her husband. She, too, had a strong desire to see justice served and focused her attention on slavery. She went as far as to purchase two South American slave plantations so that she could free the slaves and divide the land among them.

A Longtime Rivalry

France and Great Britain were on opposite sides of wars long before the 1700s. In fact, the roots of their rivalry date back as far as 1066. This was one of many reasons the French decided to come to America's aid.

Supporting the Cause

The Marquis de Lafayette was born into a wealthy family in 1757. When he was only two years old, his father was killed in battle. His mother then moved from the French countryside to Paris, leaving Lafayette's grandmother to raise him through most of his childhood. Her kind treatment of **peasants** affected the way Lafayette felt about his privileged life.

When he turned 11, Lafayette moved to Paris to be with his mother. Sadly, she passed away two years later. Lafayette was left with a large **inheritance**. At the age of 14, he followed in his family's footsteps and joined the Royal Army. When he was 16, he married a woman named Adrienne. She also came from a very wealthy and powerful French family.

Lafayette could have enjoyed his wealth and lived a life of luxury in France. However, his **morals** pushed him to do more. He heard stories about the colonists in America and believed in their cause. He felt that he needed to do something to help. Lafayette's decision to travel to the United States surprised many people.

Paris, 1777

Lafayette felt that the people fighting to form a new country were very brave. Their goal was to create a country that was free from **tyranny**. Lafayette agreed with what the colonists were trying to do. In 1777, he went to America to help the soldiers in any way he could. He knew that meant he would fight as a soldier himself. Lafayette was excited to show his bravery on the battlefield.

Help from Benjamin Franklin

Lafayette also asked several French military officers to volunteer with him. Many were eager to join him. Benjamin Franklin had come to France the year before. He had shared the struggles that the colonists faced. Many French people were interested in the Americans because of Franklin. They were impressed with him. His writings and his ideas about science made Franklin very famous in France.

The war began at the Battle of Lexington on April 19, 1775.

War Propaganda

Some of the stories of events that led up to the American Revolution were dramatized in writing and art. Both sides used **propaganda** to try to urge others to support them in the war.

Diplomacy at Its Best

Congress sent Franklin to France in 1776 to try to convince the French to accept America as its own country. The colonists needed a world power on their side. With his smarts and diplomatic skills, Franklin was able to charm France into forming an **alliance**.

Leaving France

Not all people in France were supportive of the American war. King Louis XVI did not want to be involved in America's matters. He was trying to stay **neutral** to avoid yet another war with Great Britain. He would not support a Frenchman helping the colonists. The king went as far as to issue an order that forbade French officers from serving in America. The order even mentioned Lafayette by name. Lafayette knew that if he wanted to join the war, he would have to **defy** his king.

A Ship for Sale

When Lafayette found out that the Continental Congress didn't have enough money to send him a ship, he bought his own. It was called *La Victoire*, which means "victory" in French. Lafayette was willing to use his own money and resources to join the cause!

For Love or Money

Lafayette's decision to leave France was even more of a surprise because he was not paid for any of the work he did in America. He chose to fight with the colonists for free because his desire to help was so strong.

Lafayette with the king and queen of France, Louis XVI and Marie Antoinette

Lafayette's departure for America

But Lafayette realized this was his chance to make a difference. The king did not immediately find out that Lafayette sneaked out of France and set sail for America. Lafayette felt so strongly about his decision that he left his pregnant wife and young daughter at home.

The decision to leave against orders was not easy for Lafayette. In fact, not long after setting sail, he ordered the ship to return to France. When the ship docked, Lafayette was ordered to return to his base in Marseilles. Before he could do so, a friend convinced Lafayette that going to America was the right choice. Once again, the crew prepared the ship and set sail. This time, nothing would stop them.

Lafayette in America

Lafayette was 19 years old when he arrived in America in 1777. His ship landed in South Carolina. From there, he traveled by land for a few weeks to get to Philadelphia. Even though he was young, Congress gave him the rank of major general because he was from French nobility.

It was here that Lafayette first met George Washington. Washington took him to see the military camp that was stationed just outside the city. At first, Washington was embarrassed about the condition of the camp and of his troops. The American soldiers were not as well equipped as French troops would have been. They also were not as well trained. Lafayette reassured Washington that he was there to learn, not teach.

Washington meets Lafayette in Philadelphia in 1777.

The Frenchman was in **awe** of Washington during their meeting. Washington realized that Lafayette was a good ally. A connection to an important country such as France would be helpful. However, Washington also knew that Lafayette did not have a lot of wartime experience. He invited Lafayette to live in his quarters. This was a rare invitation. Washington was impressed with the Frenchman's desire to help the colonists gain their freedom.

George Washington

Like Family

Many historians compare the bond between Lafayette and Washington to that of a father and son. Lafayette was 25 years younger than Washington and had spent much of his life without his father. He may have seen the elder American as a father figure.

In His Words

Lafayette wrote about his first meeting with Washington in his memoirs. He wrote, "General Washington came to Philadelphia, and M. de Lafayette beheld for the first time that great man. Although he was surrounded by officers and citizens, it was impossible to mistake for a moment his majestic figure."

Friends in Battle

Another young officer in Washington's camp came from the West Indies. His name was Alexander Hamilton. He had many things in common with Lafayette. They had both been orphaned at young ages. They were both strong supporters of the war. Both men held the favor of Washington. Hamilton was one of Washington's aides, which meant he was almost always nearby. Lafayette and Hamilton became friends very quickly.

Pen Pals

Lafayette and Hamilton exchanged many letters during the course of their friendship. They often shared updates about what was happening on the battlefields.

New Friends

Lafayette and Hamilton had great affection for each other. In a letter to his wife, Lafayette wrote, "Among the general's aides-de-camp is a (young) man whom I love very much and about whom I have occasionally spoken to you. That man is Colonel Hamilton."

Hamilton had recently been made an aide to Washington, a job that he was not excited to have. Hamilton would have preferred to stay on the battlefield. But Washington needed Hamilton's writing talents more than his skills in combat. Hamilton took the job because he knew that Washington would be a powerful ally to have. While Lafayette would be a leader on the front lines, Hamilton would spend most of his time on the sidelines.

Marquis de Lafayette and George Washington

Injured in Battle

Just a few months after meeting Washington, Lafayette fought in his first battle. It was September 1777, and the battle became known as the Battle of Brandywine. Lafayette was very brave, and he proved himself strong and capable.

This was a tough battle, in part because the **terrain** made it hard to know when the British were coming. There were many **fords** that the American soldiers had to block. The Americans were also outnumbered. Soon, the British troops were closing in on them. Lafayette was shot in the leg. Despite his injury, he was still able to lead a group of soldiers as they **retreated**. Soldiers were impressed that Lafayette helped get men out of the area safely given his condition.

Lafayette was rushed to a house nearby after the battle. Washington sent his own doctor to care for Lafayette. He told the doctor, "Take charge of him as if he were my son, for I love him with the same affection."

Battle of Brandywine

Lafayette leads troops into battle.

Perseverance

The Battle of Brandywine was a major loss for the Americans. Congress had to flee because the British had a clear path to the nation's capital in Philadelphia. However, the Continental Army was not ready to back down. Washington claimed "most of my men are in good spirits and still have the courage to fight the enemy another day."

Hide and Seek

Hamilton had a different task during the battle. He had to move military supplies, such as shoes, blankets, and clothing, out of Philadelphia. The British cavalry ambushed his mission, but he made a narrow escape.

Trusting a Friend

The winter of 1777–78 was very tough. Washington and his troops were camped at Valley Forge in Pennsylvania. The army had no money to properly feed or clothe its troops. Supplies were **scarce**. Many soldiers didn't even have shoes. Men died from starvation and the cold. Washington used the time away from battle to train his troops. They would come out of this winter better prepared to fight the British soldiers. Both Lafayette and Hamilton stayed at the camp and helped however they could. But not everybody supported General Washington. Some of the other officers thought he was weak and wanted to replace him.

Washington meets with Lafayette at Valley Forge.

In January 1778, the **Board of War** gave Lafayette orders to leave Washington and lead an invasion into Canada. Lafayette wasn't sure a winter attack in the far north was a strong plan of action. The weather would be brutal for the soldiers. Washington told him to go anyway, knowing that the attack would probably be called off.

Lafayette trusted his friend. He led troops as far as Albany, New York. There, he found far fewer American troops waiting for him than expected. They would most certainly face defeat. The invasion was called off. Lafayette led his troops back to Valley Forge.

In His Own Words

Lafayette was a huge supporter of Washington and spoke up for him when people talked about replacing him. "Our general is a man truly made for this revolution, which could not succeed without him."

Conway Cabal

French officer Thomas Conway led a group of military officials to try to replace Washington as the head of the Continental Army. They wanted to put General Horatio Gates, president of the Board of War, in charge. This group became known as the Conway Cabal. Lafayette was asked to join, but he refused.

Washington's Namesake

In 1779, Lafayette's wife gave birth to a son. He was named after Lafayette's most respected friend. His name was Georges Washington de Lafayette.

Hero of Two Worlds

During this stay in France, Lafayette was named Commander of the Paris National Guard. He was given the title "Hero of Two Worlds."

Back to France

Battles continued throughout 1778. Lafayette proved to be a great **asset** in the war. By the end of the year, Lafayette requested to return to France on leave. Congress approved, telling him to "return at such time as shall be most convenient to him." In February 1779, he set sail for France.

Lafayette had not left France under the best terms. He had gone to America against the king's wishes. When he returned home, he saw his family right away. Lafayette was then sent into **exile** at a hotel for eight days. He was not allowed to see anyone except for his family. Lafayette had spoken to the queen, and she was supportive of him, but the king had not talked to him about what he had done. Lafayette had to be punished for his actions.

During this time, the king learned that many people thought Lafayette's exile was not fair. The king **summoned** Lafayette and commended him on his actions in America. He was even more pleased when the Continental Congress honored Lafayette with a golden sword for his service.

King Louis XVI of France

Lafayette with his son,
Georges Washington de Lafayette

In Need of Aid

There was another important reason for Lafayette's trip to France. He wanted to gather French support for the United States. He knew that American troops needed people to fight and more supplies to win the war. Lafayette also knew that more money was needed. With more money, they could properly feed and clothe the American soldiers. The French could provide this assistance. Their help could change the course of the war. He used his influence in France to get what the United States needed.

Lafayette sailed from France to Boston in 1780.

Boston

Stealing the Furniture?

Lafayette worked hard to get help for America. A French official said, "It is fortunate for the king, that Lafayette does not take it into his head to strip Versailles of its furniture, to send to his dear Americans; as his Majesty would be unable to refuse it."

A Long Trip

The passage from France to Boston took Lafayette and his crew 38 days. It was quicker than his first trip to America when he landed in South Carolina. The first trip took more than 50 days. Lafayette used the time on his first voyage to learn English. Lafayette became fluent in less than a year!

Lafayette returned to America in 1780. He brought the money, ships, and supplies that the Americans needed. First, he sailed to Boston where he met with Washington. He then made his way to Philadelphia to meet with French officials to deliver papers to them. The colonists had just suffered the worst defeat of the war in Charleston, South Carolina. The British had captured more than 3,000 soldiers and a lot of their weaponry. The colonists were in a tough spot. The news that Lafayette had brought help gave much-needed hope to the American people.

Lafayette kept his word. He proved to be a strong supporter of the American cause. Washington felt more optimistic about future battles.

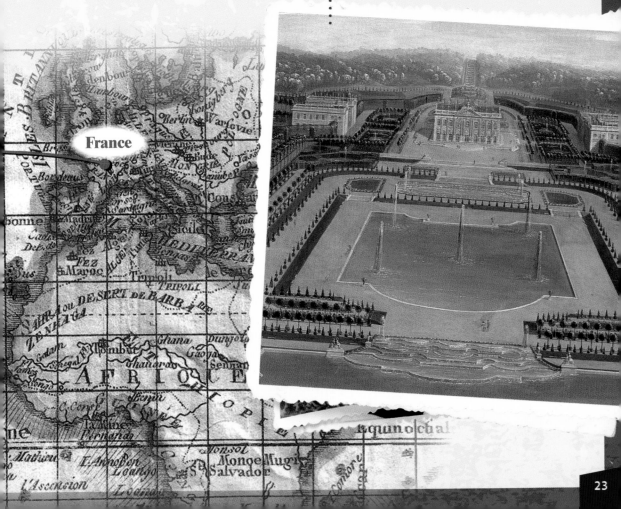

The king lived at the Palace of Versailles in France.

France

The British Surrender

Washington, Hamilton, and Lafayette worked together in one final battle at Yorktown. Hamilton had left his job as Washington's aide earlier in the year over an argument. Lafayette and Hamilton spent the next six months trying to convince Washington to let Hamilton lead troops into battle. Washington finally gave him the chance at Yorktown. Finally, Hamilton would get to join the fight. It turned out to be one of the most important battles of the Revolutionary War.

Washington used the troops and ships that had arrived from France to help in the battle. On September 28, 1781, the French ships sailed to Yorktown, Virginia. They took the British by surprise and surrounded their supply ships. Hamilton and Lafayette led the American and French soldiers on the ground. Their orders were to surround the enemy and block any path of escape. The British were trapped. The **siege** lasted for nearly three weeks. The British were forced to surrender on October 17. This was the last major battle of the war.

Alexander Hamilton

This victory would not have been possible without Lafayette's help. He had secured extra resources from France. Without them, the Americans would not have won the battle.

The British surrender at Yorktown

High Praise

Two days after the attack at Yorktown, Lafayette wrote a letter to Washington. In it, he wrote that Hamilton's "well-known talents and gallantry, were on this occasion most conspicuous and serviceable."

An Important Alliance

On December 23, 1781, Lafayette sailed home on a ship named *Alliance*. This seems a good name for a ship carrying a person who helped create a key alliance for America!

Back Home Again

After the victory at Yorktown, Lafayette returned home to France. This time, he was given a special award. It is called the Cross of St. Louis. It is only given to people who have provided a great service to the military.

Lafayette's connection to America did not end there. He came back to visit and continued to write letters to his friends in America for the rest of his life. The fighting was over in America, but there was a lot of work that needed to be done.

Cross of St. Louis

Turmoil in Europe

After his military service, Lafayette joined the French government in 1784. Years later, when the king was forced out of power, there was chaos in France. At around the same time, war broke out between France and Austria. Lafayette fled so that he would not be killed.

Lafayette did not get far. He was caught in Belgium and sent to prison in Austria for five years as a prisoner of war. Upon release, he returned home and continued to work for liberty in France.

The French Revolution was a violent time in France's history.

Jailbreak!

While Lafayette was in prison, Angelica Schuyler Church, Hamilton's sister-in-law, tried to help him escape! She and her husband, John Barker Church, came up with a plan to sneak him out in a doctor's carriage. Lafayette managed to get out of the prison but was recaptured a short time later.

Once a Friend, Always a Friend

Washington and Lafayette were friends for life. A great sign of this friendship was that young Georges Washington de Lafayette was sent to live with Washington to avoid harm while his father was in prison.

A Life of Service

Lafayette led a long life of service. Though he was a wealthy man, he worked for most of his life in either the military or government. He wanted others to have better lives. Lafayette believed that a government should represent all the people who live in a country, not just an elite few. He helped America reach that goal and worked the rest of his life to bring that dream to France. He held strong beliefs and made great efforts to share and fight for them.

Lafayette lived a **bicultural** life. He always honored his home country of France, while having a special affection for America. The bond that Lafayette formed with Washington and Hamilton continued long after the war. They wrote letters and visited each other. The words they shared reveal strong friendships and mutual respect.

PUBLIC LAW 107–209—AUG. 6, 2002   116 STAT. 931

Public Law 107–209
107th Congress

Joint Resolution

Conferring honorary citizenship of the United States posthumously on Marie Joseph Paul Yves Roche Gilbert du Motier, the Marquis de Lafayette.

Aug. 6, 2002
[S.J. Res. 13]

Whereas the United States has conferred honorary citizenship on four other occasions in more than 200 years of its independence, and honorary citizenship is and should remain an extraordinary honor not lightly conferred nor frequently granted;

Whereas Marie Joseph Paul Yves Roche Gilbert du Motier, the Marquis de Lafayette or General Lafayette, voluntarily put forth his own money and risked his life for the freedom of Americans;

Whereas the Marquis de Lafayette, by an Act of Congress, was voted to the rank of Major General;

Whereas, during the Revolutionary War, General Lafayette was wounded at the Battle of Brandywine, demonstrating bravery that forever endeared him to the American soldiers;

Whereas the Marquis de Lafayette secured the help of France to aid the United States' colonists against Great Britain;

Whereas the Marquis de Lafayette was conferred the honor of honorary citizenship by the Commonwealth of Virginia and the State of Maryland;

Whereas the Marquis de Lafayette was the first foreign dignitary to address Congress, an honor which was accorded to him upon his return to the United States in 1824;

Whereas, upon his death, both the House of Representatives and the Senate draped their chambers in black as a demonstration of respect and gratitude for his contribution to the independence of the United States;

Whereas an American flag has flown over his grave in France since his death and has not been removed, even while France was occupied by Nazi Germany during World War II; and

Whereas the Marquis de Lafayette gave aid to the United States in her time of need and is forever a symbol of freedom: Now, therefore, be it

116 STAT. 932

PUBLIC LAW 107–209—AUG. 6, 2002

Resolved by the Senate and House of Representatives of the United States of America in Congress assembled, That Marie Joseph Paul Yves Roche Gilbert du Motier, the Marquis de Lafayette, is proclaimed posthumously to be an honorary citizen of the United States of America.

Approved August 6, 2002.

This 2002 resolution restored Lafayette's honorary American citizenship.

28

American Soil

Lafayette died in 1834 at the age of 76. Soil that had been taken from his most recent trip to America covered his body. He requested that he be buried in both French and American soil to symbolize his loyalty to both countries.

Citizen or Not?

Lafayette was made an honorary citizen by each of the colonies for his service. He enjoyed this honor for the rest of his life. But, in 1935, it was ruled that his citizenship was not valid. It stayed that way until 2002, when Lafayette was finally made an honorary American citizen.

Glossary

alliance—a group that works together to reach a common goal

arranged marriage—a marriage that is planned and agreed on by the families of the bride and groom

asset—something or someone that is valuable

awe—a mixed feeling of fear, respect, and wonder

bicultural—relating to two different cultures

Board of War—a committee created to oversee the Continental Army's administration and to make recommendations regarding the army to Congress

defy—to disobey

exile—a forced period of absence from one's country or home

fords—shallow bodies of water that can be crossed by wading

inheritance—something (money, items, land, etc.) received from someone when that person dies

morals—a person's beliefs about what is right and wrong

neutral—not choosing a side in a conflict or war

peasants—poor farmers with low social status

propaganda—an organized spreading of certain ideas

retreated—withdrew from the enemy

scarce—not plentiful

siege—a type of military operation where one side surrounds a town or building, cutting off access to supplies to force those inside to surrender

summoned—called or sent for

terrain—an area of land; the physical features of that land

tyranny—a harsh or cruel government

Index

Your Turn!

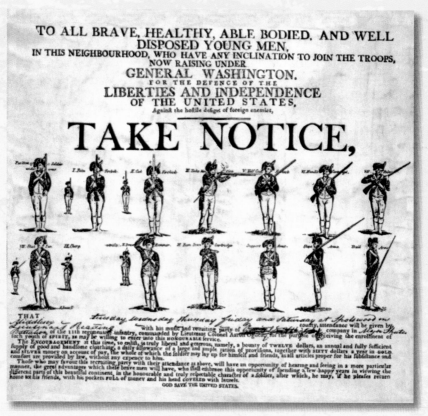

Above is a poster that was made to recruit young men into becoming soldiers in the American Revolution. The poster includes phrases such as, "To all brave, healthy, able bodied, and well disposed young men" and "he may, if he pleases return home to his friends, with his pockets full of money and his head covered in laurels." These words may make the reader want to join the cause. After studying this poster, create a response poster that highlights some of the reasons a person might NOT want to become a soldier.